HELP ME HELP MYSELF

A 30-DAY HEALING JOURNEY

Help Me Help Myself

A 30-DAY HEALING JOURNEY

JEN NICOLE

CONTENTS

I dedicate this book to all the people in the world who get up every day, trying to embrace life, in any way they see fit within their power. Being human is not always easy, hardly simple, nor predictable. It takes courage and strength to want to be a better person. Love God, love yourself, love each other, and remember that kindness is free.

There are a few select people who have impacted my life and my heart to write this book. I am grateful for each and every one of you

DAY 1

GET OVER IT

So, you are picking up this book, skimming through the first page, and probably wondering if this book can help you. You may be thinking about how a book could possibly help, but at the same time, you may be slightly curious as to what if it can. What if the answer is as simple as this: GET OVER IT! Getting over it is the miracle answer. You do not even have to continue reading through the end of the book. Just close the book now, get over it, and you're cured! Now I believe in miracles, but unfortunately, "getting over it" is not such an easy task. Family, friends, coworkers, associates, etc., may have told you just to "Get over it or "Move on." The thing is, many people would love to do just that if they just knew how to do so. Things are not always so simple. You may have tried to get over whatever pain, conflict, anger, confusion, or frustration lingering within you but have not succeeded in a breakthrough. You may have succeeded initially, or perhaps you just suppressed whatever to attempt to move forward. You may have tried to move forward and find yourself going backward. You may just be so lost that you do not know how you got to where you are. Whatever you have done up to this point has likely been your means to survive that discomfort. Whatever you have done, or wherever you are, there is still hope. You are still here so you can direct the outcome of your future. I am not here to judge you. I am not sitting here on a high horse looking down at you. I am here willing to park with you at this stage in your life as you make changes to help you help yourself. My goal is to provide you with the tools to help you heal. I am a licensed professional counselor, and I enjoy conducting therapy. However, I am not acting as your therapist or counselor in this book. I am using my expertise and skills to help you help yourself. DISCLAIMER: The information in this book is meant to enhance self-care. If you have a counselor or are seeking a counselor, do not use this book as a replacement for counseling services.

I do not know what you are particularly going through right now, but I know whatever it is, it has not killed you. There are so many things that bother us, irritate us, hurt us, disgust us, disturb us, anger us, grieve us, etc. You may be thinking, "but you have not heard my issue. I am different." You likely are different. There are billions and billions of people in this world, and we are made up of many differences. I think that is one of the things that make us special. God made no mistakes when he designed us with all these differences. However, I have learned that despite our differences, we all still endure pain. We all need time to heal. None of us are invincible. I have heard the problems and inner turmoil of many in my years here on earth. I have listened to stories as a counselor, a part of law enforcement, a military member, and just living. I do not think anything alarms me anymore. One thing is consistent: I dislike seeing people in pain.

Okay, for those people reading who just need me to be more specific to ensure that they, too, can be helped, allow me to name some common problems that people face that may or may not apply to you. You may have just recently had a loss. This loss may be in the form of death, divorce, separation, break-up, loss of custody, miscarriage, abortion, job loss, just laid off, fired, or simply quitting. Perhaps you did not have a loss, but you have another issue. Maybe you're pregnant; you just had a baby; your children are stressing you out; you're having trouble conceiving or even unable to have children. Perhaps your beloved pet died; a significant other cheated on you; someone you trusted betrayed you; you committed a crime; lost your home; are homeless; wrecked your vehicle; you're broke; spent all your money at the casino; just filed bankruptcy; your house burned down; you got assaulted; you were arrested justly or unjustly; you feel abandoned; you feel neglected; maybe you hit rock bottom; perhaps you're addicted to drugs; you're suffering from alcoholism; you cannot find your dog; your mate left you; you got robbed; your family hates you; you hate your family; you're codependent; everyone depends on you; you have nobody to rely on; you failed school; you've been diagnosed with an illness; maybe you're sick and the doctors do not have a diagnosis yet; maybe you have some regrets; you cheated on your spouse or significant other; your family disowned you; your claim was denied; you didn't get the job you applied for; you got into an accident; you got injured; you cannot make ends meet; you're being deported; you feel alone; you're afraid; you're poor; you're anxious; you're depressed; you feel misunderstood; you have no one to trust; your enemies are making life miserable for you; you cannot afford your bills; you do not like yourself; you are overweight; you're too skinny; you feel unattractive; you're overwhelmed; you do not have any help; you have no support; you are a single parent; you have no family; you have sexual issues; you have body issues; you are engulfed with insecurities; or it is something else that is distressing you. There is no way I can name every circumstance, but hopefully, this gives you some ideas of what many people struggle with. Life can be hard at times. Each person is dealt a different hand in life, so no one's life is identical to another's. I may tolerate pain differently than others. I do not heal emotionally at the same rate as another, and neither do you. Of course, some norms exist, but each person's perspective creates their own reality. Helping yourself will require you to realize that you are capable of being healed, as well as having the desire to heal. I can give you tools to help yourself, but if you choose to drown yourself in sorrow for the rest of your life, no one can stop you from doing so. You have much power, although you may not recognize it.

DAY 2

WHO ARE YOU

Who knows you better than you know yourself? Probably no one other than God. So, if you know yourself so well, what is your problem? You're reading these words and probably thinking that if I knew exactly what my problem is, I wouldn't be reading this book! Okay, okay, calm down if you are already feeling frustrated. Sometimes our problems aren't so apparent to us. We can see things plainly in others, but when it comes to ourselves, we are often blind. We may have an idea or feel like the problem is everyone else. Either way, we all have work to do within ourselves. We are all a work in progress. Others can contribute to our problems, but we must be accountable for our thoughts, attitude, and behavior. It does not excuse us even if we don't recognize our faults. We are ultimately responsible for our own well-being. Is your life filled with happiness? Is your life filled with stress? Is your life filled with disappointment? Is your life filled with sadness? Is your life filled with emptiness? Whatever your life is filled with, you are accountable. If it's filled with disappointment, then reflect on why. If it's filled with happiness, it's a reflection of your choices. Either way, you create your own temperament. If you're unhappy, please know that you can choose to be happy. You don't have to accept whatever life throws at you. You may not have control over everything and everyone in your life, but you have much control. You have enough control to create the life you want to live. Your past does not have to be your future. In fact, it shouldn't be. Each day, you are faced with new opportunities. Take advantage of these. Don't just sit there and watch your life pass you by. I like to ask the question: are you living or just existing? So, let's pause so you can reflect on the question. Please answer truthfully: **are you living or just existing?** Why just exist when God has created you to be and do so much more? There is so much to explore. There is so much to see. There is so much to learn. Life is a journey, not a race. No one is rushing to make it to old age. We may aspire to reach old age with a sound mind, but we aren't in a hurry to get there. Each day is filled with purpose. Do you have a purpose? Of course, you do... but I don't know what yours is. But perhaps you do. After all, you know you best. **So, what's your purpose?** There is no right or wrong answer. But there should be an answer. If you don't know your purpose, then perhaps it's time to discover what it is. You're probably thinking... as if I don't have enough already to do. It's not meant to be a homework assignment, but it's worth knowing. Without purpose, you're merely just growing older each year, moving about, but really going nowhere. In essence, it's like a hamster running on a wheel. The hamster is just running, although it's still in the same place! Don't be like the hamster (smile). He's confined to a cage and doesn't have the opportunity to do better. Believe me, if you open the door to the cage, that hamster is getting out of there. Often in real life, we as people have the door open wide in front of us, yet we fail to walk through it. It's a sad thing, actually. Freedom is just a few steps away, but because we fear the unknown, we don't even step out of our comfort to see what could become of this. We stay. We settle. Then we get stuck! I'm not saying this to put down people. I'm saying this to lift people. You don't have to remain stuck. But to get unstuck, you have to put forth the effort. You can't just sit there and feel sorry for yourself. Well, you can, but you'll still be stuck. You must break down the barriers to get out of the corner or come from being backed into a wall! Please do not sit or lie there waiting for someone else to do it for you. If you stay complacent there, you'll likely die there, sadly. I do not care how hard it is to get up, but I know there is something in you that is stronger than you believe. Get up and knock down the wall, and then move forward. You may have to maneuver down a different road this time: those shortcuts and other routes lead to more heartache. Don't turn back. I know it may be scary. It may even feel lonely. It may even seem too hard but push past all that. Those are just negative distortions that try to instill fear in you so that you will give up. Don't let those lies rob you of your potential. Before you fail physically, you fail mentally. It's so important to shape your perspective. It's important to build a strong mind that knows your worth. Today is your day to start equipping your mind with positivity. Today is the day that you take back your power. Today is the day that elevates you. If you ever get stuck along the way, always go back to your day one or day two. Your well-being begins in the mind. Let's do this!

DAY 3

REVISITING PURPOSE

Hey, how are you feeling today? I hope you're doing okay. If you're not, do not be afraid to seek out help. Do not be afraid to talk to someone about how you feel. Holding it in only makes it worse. Be encouraged.

So I know you're probably anxious to move on to the next thing, but remember, healing takes time. It is not something that is going to happen overnight. We do not want to move on too fast and miss the lesson. A lot of times, the stuff that I am talking about in this book can be heavy. It may take some time for you to acknowledge it, receive it, or even process it. So sometimes we will take a pause to reflect on the material given the day prior.

Yesterday the focus was on understanding your purpose. Were you able to identify what that is exactly? It is okay if you have not just yet, but perhaps it is time to start figuring it out. You are the author of your story, so it is up to you to write it. Perhaps now is a good time to start identifying goals and your plan as well. The plan and goals you decide on do not have to be permanent. Have room for some flexibility. But before you really start making life plans, it is important to at least have an idea of your purpose. What does your life mean to you? What does it mean to others? Are you running your own race and staying in your own lane? Are you a leader or a follower? What is attainable for you right now? What would be attainable for you in a year? What direction are you going? What needs to change? What needs to stay the same? What do you need at this moment? I want you to ask yourself all of these questions. It would be helpful for you to write them down and write down your answers. It is important to have a vision. Do not just be living without having anything to look forward to.

As you plan for your future, do not lose sight of the present. Do not just think that you must wait to see change in a few months. Some changes may take a couple of months, but you can start making changes now. You can also take advantage of the present. While goals and plans are good to have, it is also good not to forsake today. Today you have a lot of power. There is a lot of good if you look for it. Connect with yourself and reflect. Life is too short just to let today pass by. It still counts. What can you do today to make yourself smile? Do whatever that is while you focus on your purpose. Tune in tomorrow for something new.

DAY 4

ACCOUNTABILITY

Much of how we deal with pain is based on how we were raised and persevered through it. A lot of pain stems from unresolved childhood trauma. Although we age and grow, the pain does not magically go away. It attaches to us, and if it is not dealt with, it will manifest at some point. Then we find ourselves stuck, running in the same circle repeatedly. Does this sound familiar at all to you?

So, I ask, who are you? How did you get to where you are today? The way you function, the way you think, the way you feel, the way you act, and the way you react is not merely by accident or coincidence. I am not going to say that your behavior justifies your pain, but it may help you understand yourself. Have you been feeling misunderstood? No one seems to get you, and you may feel alone. Although you may feel misunderstood, recognize that, in general, humans are complicated! Sometimes it is difficult to understand ourselves as individuals, so how can we expect the next person to understand us? The next person has their own issues that they are wrestling with! Also, be mindful that just because you aren't aware of what another person is going through does not mean they are okay. Sometimes people hide their issues from the surface and others. Sometimes people try to hide their issues from themselves (ironically). I want you to grasp that although our feelings are very personal, let's try not to make our feelings everyone else' s problem. Why? Well, the truth is, it is not their problem! The person who can change how you feel is yourself. No other person has that power over you unless you give it up. If you give someone else your power, then you become that person's puppet. Someone else pulls your strings, and you perform. When you think about that, how does it make you feel? Why allow another person to have your power? Why be a puppet?

Now there are instances when another person may do or say something that causes one to feel a certain way. But even then, that person is not in control of you unless you relinquish your control. You can feel however you want to feel, but your actions are a reflection of you. Even when you indicate that someone has hurt your feelings, you choose to feel what you feel. You may not do so consciously, but unconsciously you do. Your feelings are often based on your thoughts, trauma, triggers, pain, history, and where you are regarding healing. For instance, if a stranger at the store was to call you ugly for no apparent reason, you may or may not be offended. However, many people would not feel hurt about what was said in general. Many may feel disrespected or even upset that this stranger dared to criticize them for nothing. Others may feel hurt or sad, although this stranger has no meaning whatsoever in their life. The people who feel hurt or sad likely have some insecurities within or have heard similar words before. It may affect them differently based on trauma and past pain. Now those who may have been offended but not sad may be confident in their looks or realize that a stranger's comment on what beauty is has no merit in one's life.

I am not advocating that people should be able to say whatever they want whenever they want or just be rude-I am simply stating that we only have control over what we say, do, and feel. In the example above, how one responds to outside stimuli (others or circumstances) is so important because whatever choice you make, you are accountable for. I am not going to tell you how you should handle people who are rude to you, but I am hoping that you will not allow them to pull your strings. That is why it is essential to have self-control and also boundaries. We will go deeper with this soon.

TODAY TAKE SOME TIME TO PONDER ON WHICH THINGS YOU need to be accountable for and what people you are accountable to. Are there some things you have not taken accountability for that perhaps you should have? Have you blamed others without even acknowledging your own part in a matter? Have you looked at yourself in the mirror and seen where you can do better? Today is a time to do better. We all have fallen short at some point, so forgive yourself and begin to do better.

DAY 5

WHAT'S ON YOUR MIND

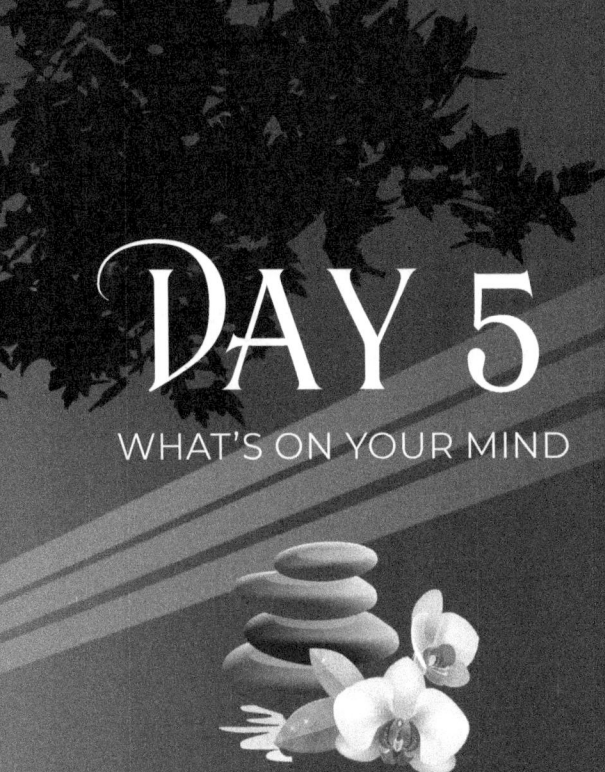

To feel better, you have to do better. Ordinarily, you just do not wake up and feel better. Usually, there is some sort of work that has to be done. You have to make an effort to feel better. I am not saying that is an easy task because, more than likely, it will not be. If so, you likely would not be reading this book.

The way you feel often is based on your thoughts. You have a thought before feeling what you feel. Your thoughts ultimately guide your feelings. If you have constant negative thoughts racing through your mind throughout the day, then you're not going to feel so good. However, if you have positive thoughts occupying your mind throughout the day, more than likely, your feelings will be a reflection of that. So be careful with your thoughts. If you constantly have negative thoughts, it is time to think differently. You are, in essence, poisoning your own self. What sense does that make?

Thoughts that put you in a bad or sad mood are draining. It sucks all the energy from you. You're not productive. You're not a joy to be around. Why spend life like this? Such ways lead to disheartening results. You will not be able to be whole if you saturate yourself with the wrong thoughts. You do have a choice on what you think. It is your own mind. Resist the urge to continue down a path of destruction. Remember, your thoughts influence your feelings. Think about things that bring life to you. Think about things that make you smile. Maybe think about the things that excite you. Think about how you can improve. Think about your goals. Think about how you can be a blessing to someone else. Think about rainbows and stars if you want to. Just fill your mind with things that do not get you down.

Now, of course, there will be times when it is necessary to confront the ugly. You may be forced to look at something that is negative, but if you do, just do not dwell in that place. Get the information you need and then determine what needs to be done to move forward.

I challenge you today to rebuke the negativity and focus on the positive things in your life. In fact, try doing this for a week and see if it makes a difference in your life. Because I am a realist, I realize that you are going to mess up. You will intend not to go to that dark place in your mind, but somehow, you'll look up and be there! If that happens, it is okay. Just guide your mind out of that place, back to where you start seeing some light. Do not give in to negative thoughts. If you allow them to do so, they will keep going and going like the energizer bunny. Those thoughts impact your feelings, and your feelings affect how you behave. It is all connected. If you find yourself having blowups often, it is because you allow your feelings to get the best of you.

While we're here, let's dig into this more (because it is important). I explained that the thought is connected to your feelings which are connected to your actions or behavior. But thoughts are not the beginning. Your beliefs influence your thoughts, guiding the feelings to which you act or react. So, before you think anything, you already have a basic belief. So that's a topic of its own. We'll touch on beliefs in the next chapter.

TODAY, THINK ABOUT WHAT NEGATIVE THOUGHTS CLOUD YOUR mind. What are some negative thoughts that just keep resurfacing? Are you able to disrupt your mind and replace them with positive thoughts? Throughout the day, are you mostly positive or mostly negative? Let's work on trying to think more positively. If you find some negative thoughts you cannot rid yourself of, perhaps it is deeper than you realize. It may be due to the belief that is under the thought. If so, this will get addressed later.

DAY 6

BELIEFS

So yesterday, we spoke about how your feelings are caused by your thoughts. I brought up that before you have thoughts, you have beliefs. So to give you an idea of how it all comes together, just understand this: BELIEFS influence your THOUGHTS which cause your FEELINGS, which ultimately guide your ACTIONS. It is all connected. It is all a process. So today, we will focus on what your beliefs are composed of. What do you believe? Who do you believe in? How did you come to that belief? Were your beliefs passed on to you through culture, family, upbringing, church, etc.? Sometimes people believe, not even realizing why they believe what they believe. Have you ever dissected your beliefs? Have you ever confronted them? Have you ever meditated on them? Have you ever found that your beliefs were based on a lie? That is deep. Sometimes we do things based on our belief, only to find that our belief is faulty. That is why it is important to know why you believe what you believe. Make sure you have your own mind and your own values. Also, do not be afraid to challenge your own beliefs to see if they are valid. Also, just because one believes something does not mean it is the absolute truth. We all have the unique ability to filter information through our own lenses. Therefore, if you have endured trauma, you may have tainted glasses. I am not implying that all who have endured trauma cannot see clearly. However, I am saying that if a person has not healed from that trauma, there will be times when the view is obstructed — this may even be unconsciously. Also, please note that this does not only apply to those who have endured trauma. Depending on the circumstances of your life, you may interpret things much differently than others. So, although something may seem one way, and you are convinced that you are accurate-you may not be in actuality.

This is why it is important not to jump to conclusions swiftly. Perhaps try to be open-minded. Hear another person out before making judgment. A lot of times, so much is a misunderstanding. People do not always perceive things the same, so getting clarification is okay. Also, do not be so afraid to agree to disagree. That is the beauty in us. We all have our own minds, beliefs, and thoughts, so it is normal to have different opinions. Just because someone thinks differently does not necessarily mean that you are right and they are wrong. Maybe no one is wrong. What if you both could be right?

TODAY FOCUS ON YOUR BELIEFS AND START TO EXAMINE THEM. Find out why you believe what you believe. Are you secure in your beliefs? Are you questioning your beliefs? Ensure that you have a good idea of why you believe what you believe, and ensure that your beliefs align with your values.

DAY 7

STARTING EACH DAY

Upon waking up each day, what is your mindset? What are your first thoughts upon waking? Do you get up feeling refreshed, or are you still tired? If you're not waking up feeling refreshed regularly, perhaps it is time for you to make some changes. Sleep is essential to your well-being. If it is not peaceful, it often sets the tone for the rest of your day. We will talk about the importance of sleep and rest later on.

Rather you had a rough night or a night filled with wonderful dreams when you start your day, how do you lead? You have the power to start the day off, good or bad. If yesterday was not a good day, then celebrate that it is a brand-new day. Don't dwell on yesterday when there is nothing you can change about what's behind. If there is something you can do today to undo a wrong, then let's do what needs to be done to move forward. You're in control of the present so take advantage of it. It is all in your thoughts. When you start the day, is your mind ready? Are you ready? How about starting the day off with faith that the day is going to be good and productive? For instance: when you awake, take time out to thank God for his grace. Starting the day off with humility and thanksgiving sets the tone. Think of three things that you're grateful for. It is an easy task and something that is not much of an inconvenience for you to do. This is how I would recommend that you start all your days. When you wake up feeling encouraged, goodness will likely continue with you. Having gratitude early in the day allows you to focus on the good instead of the bad. Thinking of what you are thankful for should put you in a good mood. Okay, okay, it should have you at least in a decent mood. Now the key is to not follow the good up with complaints, negativity, or things of that sort. Try to ease away from the negativity, for it only will drain you. Negativity in itself does not provide solutions or peace. Instead, it creates unnecessary havoc.

Now I do understand that we do not live in a perfect world. Bad things are going to happen. I'm not implying to ignore the bad or not discuss negative things. What I am saying is, don't start your day off messy! And when bad things happen, don't dwell on them. Acknowledge and deal with it (if necessary).

So, have you thought of three things you are grateful for? It is time to reflect on that. Take a moment to say out loud what you are grateful for. As you continue throughout the day, be mindful of these things. Despite whatever comes up, you have something to smile about. Try to remember to do this routine each day, perhaps thinking of something different you're thankful for rather than repeating the same things daily. As blessed as you are, there is likely much that you take for granted. Sometimes it is interesting to dig deep and recognize some of the things you value that you generally do not give notice to.

To help you with thinking of things that you are grateful for, I have chosen to share some of mine.

I am thankful that I am of sound mind.
I am thankful that I am breathing.
I am thankful that I have eyes to see.
I am thankful I am able to taste and enjoy food.
I am thankful that I have my freedom.
I am thankful that I have clean water to drink.
I am thankful for my family.
I am thankful for the mercy of God.
I am thankful for kindness.
I am thankful for wisdom.
I am thankful for all of you.

DAY 8

BOUNDARIES

Don't run from your problems. Address them instead. If you keep running, you will find that you will always be running, for your problems will keep chasing you. Failing to address them does not erase them. They just instill fear in you. Whatever it is, know that you can handle it. Stop running. Address it head-on, responsibly. If you don't feel strong enough to address it alone, bring in reinforcement.

Your reinforcements are the people on your team. Who is on your team? Who can you trust? Who can you confide in? This is who you want at your side when you feel you need help. Please just don't get anyone for this task. Selecting anyone can be a setback. Not everyone wants what is best for you. Not everyone who is around you loves you. Not everyone around you is supportive. Not everyone around you wants to see you win. In fact, some of the people around you may need to get away from you. Don't wait for them to remove themselves from your life: kindly do it for them. You don't want to carry around dead weight. You need people around who are invested in you. You need people around you that have value. You need people around who complement your qualities. You want people around who genuinely want the best for you. Perhaps today is a time to start being positive and around people who are like-minded.

You may find that some people are draining your energy. Sometimes it is that they are takers. Sometimes it is that they are miserable. Sometimes it may be that you enable them. Whatever it is, this is not healthy for you. Perhaps you do not have to put them out of your life completely. Perhaps you just need to put up a fence. I like to think of boundaries as fences. It is something you put up to protect your peace and well-being. Think of it like this: if you do not keep a gate up in your yard, what is stopping a stray dog from crapping in your yard? By installing a fence, you minimize unwanted strays or people from getting too close to your home. So, think of boundaries in the same way. You implement boundaries to keep people at a distance. It is a means of protecting you. We all must have personal boundaries (limitations a person sets for themselves in interpersonal relationships). Boundaries can be healthy, rigid, or porous. If you have difficulty saying no to others, you likely do not have healthy boundaries. I am not advocating that it is healthy to say no generally, but I am implying that one should not generally feel guilty about wanting to say no to something they do not want to do. A person with healthy boundaries is comfortable sharing personal information with others appropriately. A person with healthy boundaries is confident in their values and is not swayed by others. A person with healthy boundaries communicates what they need. A person with healthy boundaries is not afraid to say no or hear no.

If you are a person who overshares information or is often found meddling in the affairs of others, who needs validation from others, or who generally gets misused and mistreated, you likely have some porous boundaries. If you're a person who often avoids intimacy with others, or you are very fearful of rejection or not comfortable receiving help from others, you may have some rigid boundaries.

Take some time today to reexamine your relationships. Do you need to implement boundaries that you have not? Sometimes people are good at setting boundaries with certain people but may find it difficult to do with others, depending on the closeness of the relationship. For instance, one may have good boundaries at work but be terrible at setting boundaries with family. Yes, boundaries do not just have to be with people. It could be something like your job and time that you have to set limits with.

Remember, the gate is for you to put up, so you can have more control over what gets your energy. Suppose your friend calls you daily venting, and although you want to be a good friend, you feel like this is draining your energy. So maybe you have to tell your friend that you cannot talk the next time they call. Maybe you're comfortable being honest and can say you want to be supportive, but the venting sessions are not really that helpful. Perhaps, in this case, you may suggest your friend try therapy or even get a journal to minimize these venting sessions. For some, this may seem cruel, but in actuality, it is not. Listening to the same person vent daily is unhealthy for either of you. The venting is not helping the problem. Now, sometimes venting is helpful (for sometimes people just need an outlet), but not if this is an everyday occurrence. If you have a friend who refuses to stop venting to you, you still have options. Maybe you stop answering the phone, or maybe you keep calls short. It is important that you enforce your boundaries. If you choose to allow others to disrupt your peace because you did not put up the gate, then you are the problem. Sorry, I am just being frank. Sometimes the truth hurts.

I know the truth can sometimes hurt because I am human too. I was a person who said yes often. I am naturally compassionate and kind, so I usually did what people asked of me (as long as it did not go against my values). I found that I was a revolving door; people knew I was kind, so they continuously asked me for favors. These were not people who often did favors for me, or really ever. I was just a nice person. But as nice and kind as I was, I often felt overwhelmed. I had to tend to my own affairs and help everyone else too. There was a point when I felt so weak because it was hard to keep up. Then one day, this coworker of mine, who everyone knew to be selfish, shared some information with me. He said it was my fault that I was so overwhelmed. I wasn't complaining to him, but I guess he saw that I was struggling. He told me he enjoyed his life, and that was merely because he did not do favors for others. He said he usually said no to others and concentrated on his own affairs. When he told me that, I thought to myself, "I was right, he is so selfish." But, the more I thought about it, I began to understand why he told me being overwhelmed was my fault. Honestly, I was silently frustrated with people asking me for help. But he told me it was my fault. Then it finally made sense. It was my fault because I did not have to say yes when others asked things of me. What was stopping me from saying no? I did not want to hurt their feelings, or I felt sorry for them. But who was feeling sorry for me? It was not their responsibility to see if I had too much on my plate. It was my own. I realized that

I had not implemented boundaries that protected me from being overwhelmed. I did not have healthy boundaries at all. I had to listen to my own needs and wants. I had to prioritize what was important to me. I had to start telling people no. I admit it was not easy initially. It took time for me to start standing up for myself because there was pushback. But that is when I really realized that some people just did not care about me at all. It was all about what I could do for them. My eyes were opened to who people really were.

I challenge you today to see what you need to do differently. You may not be able to implement healthy boundaries all at once, but at least start. Determine the areas where you feel overwhelmed. Are you spending too much time at work? I do not mean the standard working hours. Are you doing more than your fair share? Are you staying at work late, not even being compensated? Are you taking your lunch break? Are you taking your other work breaks? Are you taking work home with you instead of ending the work day when you leave? Are your friends and family taking too much of your time? Are they frustrating you with demands and making you feel guilty? Are you stretched so thin that you do not even have time for yourself? Are you sacrificing your personal time too often to help others? Are you giving and giving and not recuperating? Are there responsibilities that can be delegated or shared? Is it your responsibility to care for everyone and everything, or have you just been the designee? What areas need to be tended to so that you can have peace?

DAY 9

CHECK IN

Hey, you. How are you doing? I felt after a little over a week of starting a journey to healing where you are doing the work by yourself, perhaps I should have you pause to just see where you are mentally and emotionally. Maybe you are doing okay and ready to just keep it moving. You are not at the point where you think it is time to rest or take a few breaths. If this is where you are, I am proud of you. More importantly, you should be proud of yourself for pushing through and getting through your first week. In fact, even if you are not feeling so good about this journey, I want you to be proud of yourself for getting this far. Healing takes time. It is a journey and not a race.

Now that you can still be proud of yourself, take this moment to pause and reflect on what you read last week. Are there any days you need to refer back to? If so, it is okay. I actually would recommend you to do so. Sometimes we do not absorb everything at once. Sometimes we forget everything we just read. Maybe you have not forgotten, but you found something helpful and want to meditate on it. Do what works for you.

If you are in a place where you find yourself struggling just because life has happened, my heart pours out to you. It is difficult to endure challenge after challenge. Sometimes it seems that life beats you up all at once. You cannot even get a breath in before something else happens. Maybe that is not the issue with you. Maybe you are hurting so bad, and the pain will not let up. It seems that maybe you can distract yourself for a moment, but that pain just sits and waits for you. So really, there is no real escape. You may feel drained, frustrated, afraid, sad, or angry, and really do not know how to feel any other emotion right now. You may feel overwhelmed by your present stressors. You may be thinking life is so unfair. Whatever it is, just know that the pain is temporary. It is not forever, although it feels like it is. When you are in a storm, it is hard to see what is on the other side. It is so hard to see through all the hail, dark clouds, and debris. But hang in there, do not give in to the pain. Do not let it destroy you. Do not start thinking negatively; if you already are, it is time to stop. You can beat this pain. You are stronger than you know. Push past the discomfort and know that you have a purpose.

Take time to rest today. You can get back to doing the hard stuff tomorrow. Be encouraged.

DAY 10

WHAT'S BEEN COVERED SO FAR

Healing is definitely a journey; remember, all you need to do is take it one day at a time. You cannot rush it, although you want to. Essentially, we just want to feel better. We are tired of hurting, feeling frustrated, starting over, feeling lost, etc. We just want to be at a place where we can feel whole. We want to feel well and excited about life. We want joy. We want peace. Why is life difficult at times? Why is life unfair at times? So many questions, but not enough answers. I get it. That is why I am trying to help you help yourself. Give yourself some grace in this journey. If you do not, you just add more pain to the process. I often say we are all a work in progress. Although we are so different, all of our pain hurts. We all bleed red. Know that you are not alone in how you feel. Somedays, you may feel good. On other days, you may feel like the entire world is against you. Whatever you're feeling, just know you are not abnormal.

can be like a rollercoaster. They go up and down. There will be highs, and there will be lows. But aim for the highs and do not give up on yourself. Keep going, no matter how slow the progress. Just do not stop. You're alive, so you have another chance to get it right. You may mess up along the way. In fact, you will mess up along the way. There are no perfect people. As good as a person that I am, I too, fall short sometimes. It is life. Just accept it and press on. Be encouraged.

So you have made it to day ten in your self-healing journey. A lot was covered in such a short time. So do not expect you're good now just because it was covered. It will take effort and work to get better, along with time. So far, we have covered that getting over your issues will not happen overnight. We all struggle with something and depending on how deep it is, it may take ample time. No matter how long it takes, it is important not to abort the healing process. Do not fight healing. When you are met with resistance, push through. Sometimes it is life's challenges that hinder us. Sometimes it is our own stubbornness and ignorance that make things more challenging. Sometimes it is our lack of faith and motivation that deters us. Sometimes there are various distractions. Sometimes it is fear that keeps us from progressing. Most do not like being uncomfortable. So, when they start feeling uncomfortable, they find it easier to return to what is comfortable. Some people give up too easily or give up right before the breakthrough. Don't give in. Keep going.

In the first few chapters, we discussed who you are and how you came to be you. Perhaps this discussion needs to continue because you still have some things to figure out. Maybe you had a vision, and now things have changed, and you find it difficult to get back on track. Maybe it is time to create a new vision or adjust your old one. Do not be afraid to rediscover who you are or rewrite who you are. You are the author of your own narrative. Why just exist when you can live?

We covered that you are accountable for yourself. You should not be thirty years old and still be blaming everything that went wrong in your life on your upbringing. Perhaps you did have a terrible childhood, but that does not mean you're destined for a terrible adulthood. You have a choice in the matter. You are only defined by yesterday if you allow that to lead you. Learn from your past. Use your pain to strengthen you. It does not have to define you. If your past is something you cannot get past, I recommend dealing with it in therapy as a start. It is not healthy to keep pushing down things that hurt you. You can only suppress for so long.

Remember to lead with positive thoughts. Wake up with gratitude. Remember that your beliefs will influence your thoughts, which sway your feelings and guide your actions. How you feel is up to you. You have more power than you realize. How do you think your day will unfold if you fill your mind with negativity? Negativity begets negativity. You do not have to focus on the negative. You do not have to wait for bad things to happen. Bad things happen in life, and when they come, your response is your power. Often your response has much influence on the overall outcome.

Lastly, we discussed boundaries and how protecting your peace is important. You do not have to entertain everything and everyone. It is your responsibility to take care of yourself.

DAY 11

DEPRESSION

How are you doing? Have you been feeling or experiencing any of the following: apathy, discontentment, hopelessness, sadness, loss of pleasure in things you normally liked, irritability, crying a lot, isolation from others, sleep disturbances, fatigue, poor appetite, or a lack of concentration? If you have been experiencing any of the following symptoms and they seem to linger, you may be experiencing symptoms of depression. Do not be startled. These symptoms could also be the result of other factors. However, know that depression is not rare. If you are experiencing symptoms of depression, try not to be alarmed. It is serious, but it can be healed.

As a counselor, I am very familiar with depression. Depression is very common. An alarming number of individuals are faced with depression daily. It is very disheartening that so many people fall victim to such a painful mood disorder. I view depression as poison. It steals one's joy, one's peace, one's energy, one's friends, and one's mindset. The ultimate goal of depression is to isolate you from everything and everyone you love. After it does that, it consumes you and breaks you down piece by piece. It destroys you from the inside until there is nothing left. Once one is there, often a person feels like death is the only option and therefore attempts to take their own life. Even if one does not get that entangled with depression to the point where they are contemplating suicide, it is just awful to experience or endure.

Unfortunately, I have even been trapped in the web of depression. While you may frown that a counselor has had depression, it is merely the truth. No one is above it. It was not something I invited into my life. It kind of just showed up, and then it did not want to leave. I think it first took me a moment to acknowledge that it was even there. While I was familiar with depression through all my schooling and counseling experiences, I did not quite identify it when it found me. I was just trying to do my best and live my life. But depression made it difficult for me to live life normally. While you may have progressed in some areas, you may be struggling in others. Some depressed folks are very functional but suffer in silence.

If you are experiencing depression in any form, I urge you to seek help. I urge you to seek help as soon as possible. Do not give it time to manifest in other areas of your life or to become worse. Get a hold of it. Like me, it may first take for you to acknowledge what it is. Having it does not mean you're weak. Sometimes the preconceptions keep us in denial or hinder us from seeking help. There is no shame in getting help. We all need help sometimes.

You may be wondering what help is out there for depression. Well, there is evidenced based research that therapy works. As a counselor, I encourage therapy. I think it is good to have a place to unload your troubles. Therapy offers a safe place for one to vent, talk through their challenges, or even just feel heard. A counselor or therapist can offer insight to help you navigate your challenges. One can help you create goals aimed at conquering your burdens. A counselor or therapist can offer tools to help one cope as well. If you have never been to therapy, you may feel uncomfortable. It is okay to feel uncomfortable or uneasy. After all, you're sharing your heart or concerns with a stranger. But although you may feel uneasy, know that as you build rapport with your counselor, you'll start to feel at ease. Know that therapy is a place where there should be no judgment. Therapy is there to help you. If you are open to being helped, it is worth a try. Also, know that every counselor or therapist has different approaches, backgrounds, skills, etc., so if one is not a good fit, do not be afraid to try another. Please do not give up on therapy based on a bad experience. If you have had a bad experience, do not hesitate to speak with your new therapist about your feelings.

Perhaps therapy is not for you at this moment. You may find meditation to help ground yourself and help to relieve some of your depressive symptoms. It has worked for some. Journaling is another thing that some people may find helpful. Having a healthy outlet to let go of what you're holding in would be helpful. Perhaps journaling itself will not rid you of depression, but it may help with coping.

Another thing that has been helpful for many people in combating depression is medicine. Prescriptions like Prozac have been successful in altering the mood of people. It does take weeks before one notices the benefits, though. If you're open to trying it out, perhaps make an appointment with your doctor to get more information.

Exercise helps combat some symptoms of depression. Exercise is good for releasing happy endorphins within your body. This requires a routine, not just exercising sparsely. Perhaps make exercise a habit if it is healthy for you to do so. A habit does not mean every day. Maybe you are not committed to working out daily, but you can commit to three times a week. Do what is doable for you.

It is important that you do your part in fighting back against depression. Your life matters. It is imperative that you check in with somebody. Let someone else know what is going on. You do not have to keep this a secret. Remember, it is nothing to be ashamed of. You're not alone. Do not choose to suffer alone.

DAY 12

ANXIETY

Anxiety symptoms often include feeling restless, nervous, and fearful of impending mishaps or danger. One may experience trouble sleeping, intense thoughts, and intense feelings. One may have difficulty concentrating or breathing. We all experience anxiety at some point. Some anxiety is okay when it is minimal. However, if anxiety is experienced throughout your normal daily routine, perhaps it is time to do something about it. Intensive worrying and fearing about what is to come is draining and impacts your health. Anxiety interferes with normal functioning. Some people avoid people or places due to feelings of anxiety. There are several types of anxiety disorders.

If you are currently battling anxiety, know that you can get it under control. Therapy and or prescribed medicine

In the meantime, there are things that you can work on to help with your anxiety. Understanding that anxiety is essentially fear disguised as something else. When a person indicates that they are anxious, I often ask: "What are you afraid of?" There is usually some sort of fear behind those anxious thoughts or feelings. If you are willing to first determine what that underlying fear is, then you're headed in the right direction. Once you can identify the fear, try to figure out if there is anything you can do about it. If there is something you can do about it, then you have the opportunity to change the outcome. If there is nothing you can do about what you fear, then maybe it is time for you to accept that you have no control over what happens. Accepting what you can control and letting go of what you cannot do will give you some peace. For me, I like to give what I cannot control to God. In my experience, people who suffer from anxiety mostly deal with fear and control. Too often, we want to control everything we want, but in actuality, that is not life. We do not have that much power. While we do have a lot of power over ourselves, we do not have power over others and some circumstances. If you accept that, you will have a less stressful life. Stop fighting against what you cannot control.

When people worry about what might happen or what could happen, it really is not productive. Allow me to explain. How is worrying helping you? Really, please think about it. Worrying does not help anybody. Let's suppose something you worried about really did happen; why not just let what happens happen, then respond to it? Why fill your mind and heart with heaviness twice? All the time you spend worrying drains you and has you in not such a good place. Then if something actually happens, you will feel the heaviness in response to what happened. Let's suppose what you fear happening does not even happen! What benefit would you get from worrying about nothing? Are you just practicing for doom? Why not just wait and see what happens because, often, what one fears happening doesn't even happen the way one envisioned? If you can identify the fear, you can determine what can be done so that doom does not occur if it is in your control. For instance: Terrence is currently in college and has been experiencing so much anxiety this week. Terrence identifies that his anxiety is in response to his professor informing him that finals are less than a month away and will be worth half of one's final grade. Terrence has been so worried about failing the test, which would likely mean he would fail the class. In this scenario, I would urge Terrence not to worry. Worrying only adds additional stress. It is not helping him. I would suggest to Terrence that instead of worrying, he just prepares as best he can for the final. He has the power to pass the test if he studies for it. If he chooses not to study, he chooses the likelihood of failing. I would want Terrence to see that there is no need to fear a test that he can definitely pass. He is only anxious because he feels unprepared. Doing something about his insecurity puts him in a better position to succeed.

Now let's try a different scenario. Toni loves her grandparents. They are both in their early nineties, and she has so much anxiety over losing them. She just wishes they could be in her life forever. Knowing their age and health, she fears she could lose them any day. Toni's anxiety is debilitating. She finds that her anxiety is really affecting her well-being. Toni recently began therapy to address her anxiety. She enjoys being able to share with her therapist her fears as well as just good memories. Toni's therapist encourages her to take advantage of the moment, devoting her time to enjoying her grandparents while they are here. She also encourages Toni not to dread and focus on death but to accept that death happens and Toni cannot control the fate of her grandparents. Toni's grandparents are well taken care of and safe. They are not worried about death and happy to enjoy the present. Toni now spends more of her free time visiting her grandparents or talking to them on the telephone. Toni is working through accepting and letting go of what she cannot control. Her doing so has helped minimize her anxiety. It is not all gone, but Toni feels so much better.

Know that anxiety does not have to control you: you have to control it. Identify that fear and confront it. Do not waste your time being drained by circumstances that may or may not happen. If you have control, do something about it. If you do not, let go and accept that there is nothing you can do. If there is nothing you can do, there is nothing to feel guilty about. We all have limitations. Be encouraged.

I understand that while this information is beneficial, you may not be able to sort through it all at once. I have listed some things to help you cope or calm yourself when anxiety arises. Try to verbalize how your thoughts, feelings, and behavior contribute to you being anxious. Ponder if you are greatly concerned about threats that are unrealistic. Also be mindful that avoiding your fears may heighten your fear, which will prolong your anxiety. You can manage anxiety symptoms by doing muscle relaxation, guided imagery, slow breathing (inhaling slowly, and then exhaling slowly repeatedly), and or counting to 30 to calm yourself.

DAY 13

THE INNER CHILD

We all have an inner child that lives inside of us. You may be grown, but that little boy or girl still lives deep inside. Sometimes they will surface, especially when they are triggered. Many people ignore the child within. Many people deny the child within. If you have ever suffered any trauma as a child and have not completely healed from it, that child inside still cries. That child inside still wants to be comforted.

Many people do not have any insight into the inner child without it being drawn out. It may be something many aren't familiar with because they feel that it is history, and because they survived, they must have healed. Survival does not equal healing. Many of us survive because we want to live. Many of us aren't really given a choice on what to do, so as kids, we naturally survive because kids are great at being resilient. They survive all that has happened only to become adults with a lot of suppressed pain. The problem with suppressed pain is that it will eventually resurface. This may show up as abandonment issues, poor attachment styles, post-traumatic stress disorder, poor boundaries, promiscuity, excessive anger, bad parenting, and so forth. It may manifest differently in individuals.

Let me provide a fictional but likely example of how the inner child manifests in adulthood: Nicole lived with her mother and father as a little girl. She adored them both. Nicole's parents began to have a troubled relationship shortly after Nicole turned seven. Despite the tension, they decided to remain together. A few years later, after a heated argument, Nicole's father left and never returned. He abandoned Nicole and her mother. Nicole took her father's leaving very hard. It did not make sense why he would just leave them. Nicole's mother struggled initially, but she somehow raised Nicole alone. Nicole seemed to thrive despite her upbringing. Now at 30, Nicole finds herself in therapy, feeling broken after another failed relationship with her most recent boyfriend. Nicole shared in therapy that she either has a difficult time committing, is often angry or sad within the relationship, or ends up having the worst breakups. She finds herself in a deep depression after any serious relationship. In therapy, her counselor explores Nicole's inner child and learns that Nicole is suffering from feeling abandoned. The counselor connects Nicole's father's departure with her fearing abandonment in romantic relationships. Although Nicole is now 30, the little ten-year-old girl who her father left still yearns. So when Nicole gets into a disagreement with a partner, she instantly feels anxious, afraid, and angry. She projects those feelings. Until that little girl inside of her is comforted, Nicole is going to keep encountering the fear of abandonment by her current love interests.

Perhaps something from your childhood still bothers you. Maybe something still hurts. What does that child need? Does that child need a voice? Does that child need to forgive? Does that child need closure? Does that child need a hug? What does that child inside you need to become whole? Whatever it is, it likely is worth the work. Therapy is a great place to have help with doing that work. Be encouraged.

DAY 14

TRIGGERS

We all have been susceptible to triggers. Triggers are those things said or done to you that elicit very strong negative emotions within you. Those negative emotions stem from previous experiences. It is important to be aware of your triggers. It is hard to heal when you do not understand what invokes such negative feelings. It is hard to work through triggers that have not been identified.

So you may be wondering how you can identify your triggers. Well, I would encourage you to pay attention to what normally dampers your mood or causes strong, intense negative emotions. A lot of times, people like to blame others for their triggers. You can blame all you want, but let me assure you, others are not the problem: you are. I am not implying it is okay for others to treat you harshly or be disrespectful. I only want you to acknowledge that you have to take responsibility for your triggers. Others cannot control you. They may try to get a rise out of you, but you have to learn to control your emotions and reactions. I am not even implying that your triggers or pain are not valid. I am only putting the power back into you. Now when you're in a close relationship with someone, if you share your triggers with them in the healing process, they can try to do things to lessen the likelihood of you being triggered. But even then, you are still responsible for yourself.

A lot of times, we are triggered because something happens that reinforces past pain. It may be a memory invoked. It could be fear. It could be reliving the pain or feeling its familiarity. We are human, so we are going to feel emotions. Some things will cause more pain than others, based on one's experiences. I read somewhere that "Our perspectives are filtered through our pain." I happen to agree. Let me try to explain. Let's say we all started with a clean slate—our perspective and worldview are so optimistic and delightful. The picture is clear, with no cloudiness. But then, one day, something awful happens to a person. That innocence of the world and all the goodness is now tainted based on what that person has now seen. As life happens, more good happens as well as some bad things. The more things that happen shape a person's reality. The longer they live, they begin to find different survival methods to cope. They no longer see the world as this big beautiful place full of rainbows and roses. Some people can accept that both good and bad things are essential to living, and they still are optimistic. Some people become more guarded, disconnected, or even fearful. Based on what one has individually experienced, one may see something totally different than the next person. For instance, you can have two people look at the situation and perceive it differently. Is one person lying and the next one telling the truth? Well, not necessarily. Although their recollections may vary, they may both be telling their own truth. How can they have different specifics but both be telling the truth? Because they each filter it through their own lens!

I share a method that has helped many people who struggle with triggers during the healing process. Challenge the faulty belief. You do this by writing out everything people have said that hurt you. Then after your list is complete, take some time and determine what has truth and what doesn't. You do not have to explain why it is the truth or not. At this point, you just need to separate the truths from the lies. So there may be some things that have been said to you that really hurt. Lies can hurt, but so can the truth sometimes. If you find that something has truth, that is okay. Do not get all worked up over it. Instead, determine if you're okay with the truth. If you are, then why does it trigger such negative emotions? If you find that you're accepting of the truth but still bothered, it is time to do something about that truth. What can you do to change the outcome of whatever it is about the truth that you do not like? You may not have the answer right away. That is fine. It is okay to take your time to find a resolution. Now, if you identify what has been said to you as untrue, then I ask you again: why is it negatively affecting you? What about the lie holds you hostage? Why does it matter if it is not true? Why are you entertaining lies or the people that tell them?

I want to illustrate how to tackle the task of challenging the faulty belief that causes you to be triggered. Let's suppose when compiling your list of things that have been said or done to hurt you, you come up with this:

"I've overheard someone saying I was fat." Okay, first thing first, do you consider yourself to be fat? Let's suppose the answer is yes. So, in essence, you were hurt when someone called you fat, but you actually agree. Now it is not polite for someone to say this to you, so I am not advocating that such words are okay. So perhaps you are upset and even hurt that someone was rude and called you fat when they were unaware you heard them. Ask yourself, are you mad at the person, or are you really mad at your present circumstances? If you are not okay with being obese, then do something about it. Do not just become a victim and sit in your pain. Make healthier choices, research better habits, talk to your doctor, and enlist in exercising if it is safe for you to do so. Know that you have the power to control your circumstances. You will not feel as triggered when you feel empowered. When you know that you are doing what you need to do to take care of yourself, those high emotions kind of halt. You likely won't feel as hurt when someone is rude to you.

So work on the things that trigger you. This is something that you can get under control if you work at it.

DAY 15

HEARTBREAK

If you've ever experienced having your heart broken, you remember the pain vividly. When experiencing heartbreak, you may feel like it is the worst pain in the world. If you have healed from heartbreak, then it is okay for you to skip this chapter. Take the day off and tune into the book tomorrow (smile).

If you are currently suffering the pain of having your heart broken or maybe even experienced a recent breakup, in particular, my heart pours out to you. I know your heart hurts, and this season just feels too painful. Although it feels like this pain will last forever, trust that the heart can heal in time. You'll probably not be healed by tomorrow, this week, or even this month, but the pain will hurt a little less as time passes. I cannot even say that the pain will completely ever go away. For some, it will, and for others, it may not. But in the meantime, just take it one day at a time. You may be feeling so sad, torn, confused, guilty, devastated, angry, or even numb. Whatever you're feeling, permit yourself to feel it. Do not try to deny what you feel. Let it out so you can grieve properly. It is hard to let go of someone when you still hold onto all those bottled-up emotions. That is exactly what I mean when I say feel what you feel. I do not mean to act on what you feel. Right now, you're in a very vulnerable state, and your mind is likely clouded. It is not a good idea to let your emotions have their way. It is not a good idea to give in to your emotions. But it is okay to feel them. If you need to cry, then cry. If you need to scream, scream. If you need to hit something, get a punching bag. If you need time alone, take it. If you need to talk to someone, choose a person you trust to talk to.

Breakups affect each person differently. One may just try to be distracted, so they do not have to face what is happening. Some people choose to isolate themselves. Some people feel better being surrounded by people they love. Some people overeat to compensate. Some people try to do things to numb the pain. Distracting may work for so long. Numbing only works for so long. Neither heals, just delays. Do not put your pain off: deal with it now to get past it.

After a breakup or feeling heartbroken, understand that while you may feel fine one moment, you will also have moments when you do not feel fine. You may be feeling like you're literally on an emotional rollercoaster. That is okay. You may be wrestling with why. You may be wrestling with the pain of your vision not manifesting as you wanted it to. You may be wrestling with feelings of judgment, rejection, or even guilt. You may be rehearsing everything that happened in the relationship. You may be confused about how you ended up here. Please know that you are not abnormal. Sometimes you may feel like you're going crazy. You are likely not going crazy. Do not let your mind trick you. Be careful of your thoughts. Remember, negative thoughts lead you into a dark place. If you're in that dark place, come out of it. Remember not to let the poison suck you in.

You may be feeling overwhelmed or like this is all just too much. You may be feeling like you're not deserving of what has happened. Whatever has happened has happened, and you cannot change that. You can reflect on the relationship and find where you may have contributed to the bad parts of it. It cannot be all of your partner's fault. In any relationship, no one is perfect. I am not telling you to condemn yourself-there is no good in that. But find a place where you can grow from. Find out what you can do better or differently. It may be too late for your most recent relationship, but do not let that deter you from all the good that can come in a new relationship when it is time.

While breakups are sad for many, know that this is not the end for you. You can find love again. Know that it is important to heal before you find love again. Failing to heal first will cause you to bring baggage from the old relationship into the new one. You'll transfer the pain. You'll continue in a vicious cycle. Save yourself additional heartbreak by permitting yourself to grieve the loss and heal.

DAY 16

SELF-CARE

I hope that you remember to take good care of yourself daily. It is likely that you remember to do the usual things like brushing your teeth, washing your face, taking a shower, eating, combing your hair, and grooming (I hope…lol). But too often, too many of us forget about other important things like taking time out to enjoy ourselves, having fun, laughing, and spending time with people we love and care about. Some of us have virtually turned into human forms of robots. We have the same routine from day to day. We have become so predictable. Nothing about us is even exciting anymore. We may not even remember the last time we had fun or even what we liked to do for fun. We have been accustomed to being responsible by doing things like working, paying bills, taking care of children and others who depend on us, eating food just to survive, going to sleep because we're tired, and starting the next day to do it all over again. That is not living.

but existing. I challenge you to break this vicious cycle if this has become you. I challenge you to bring some excitement into your life again by living and making yourself a priority again. I am not suggesting abandoning everything else, but making yourself and what is important to you a priority from this week forward.

Self-care is about taking time out to do what you need to do so that you are emotionally, mentally, and physically sound. Self-care allows you to recenter or regroup. It gives you the time to give back to yourself. It is so important that this is not neglected. When self-care is neglected, you ultimately pay the price in some form. The absence of self-care leaves one open to depression, anxiety, fatigue, stress, and much more.

Self-care can be sleep, rest, a massage, a long bubble bath, alone time, going out, meditation, having fun, exercising, enjoying nature, or maybe doing absolutely nothing at all. Self-care may look different for each of us. You know what you need. You know what needs to be tended to within you. Do not allow distractions to keep you from taking care of yourself. Remember that you are accountable for yourself. If you do not do the required maintenance, then at some point, you are going to have some big problems. You can think of our bodies like a car. The car needs certain things to allow it to run. We, as people, need certain things to get going. Sometimes we are riding on empty, but still pouring out to others. We are empty and giving what we do not even have. A car on empty can only keep rolling for so long. Eventually, it is going to come to a complete stop. As a human, if you refuse to refuel, you, too, will come to a stop. It is going to drain and consume you. You will likely feel ready to shut down. You're likely irritable, upset, and tired. You're probably not as pleasant as you usually are. You may become ill.

Your mental, spiritual, emotional, and physical well-being should be important to you. All these components work together to make you who you are. Self-care keeps these things balanced and thriving. The absence of self-care means you will suffer in at least one of these areas. Why suffer unnecessarily? If there are things that you can do to ensure your self-care is intact, what is stopping you? Some may say that they are too busy. How are you too busy for yourself? How does everything else come before you? It is some things that should be sacrificed-but self-care should not be it. If you are down, you cannot help yourself or anyone else. Make yourself a priority if you have not. You do not have to be arrogant when doing so, but this is a time when you must be a little selfish. If not, you'll take self-care for granted.

I encourage you today to get motivated about tending to yourself. I encourage you to take your own well-being very seriously. Think about what you eat, what you drink, how active you are, if you are having fun, if you get enough rest, if you have support, and where your peace is. Also, please do not neglect your sleep or rest. It is important. Your body needs to reset itself, and it does so when you are sleeping. If you are not getting proper rest, your body may not have time to thrive, repair, or recenter itself. Listen to your body, and cater to it. Find ways to take care of yourself, and make yourself a priority. You're so worth it!

DAY 17

CHECK-IN

Wow, you have surpassed a little more than two weeks. At this point, you have less than two weeks to go! How are you feeling? Are you still motivated? Are you excited about your healing journey? Have you learned some interesting things about yourself in this process? I hope so. I hope you're not giving up on yourself. I hope that you are motivated to continue and press forward.

As we approach a new week, I want to remind you of what we covered this last week. It was so much information, and I hope you retained it. We discussed the feelings of depression and anxiety. We discussed ways to overcome them. Once again, remember that your experience may not be another's experience, and so on. Do not minimize your symptoms based on the criteria of someone else. You're entitled to experience your own path. It will look different in some regard, and that is okay.

We discussed the inner child, boundaries, triggers, and heartbreak. We also discussed self-care. I hope you envision self-care as a treat that does not have to be earned. It is just a need, just like your body needs water. So what are you doing today? If you can, please use today to find a way to engage in some self-care. Do not put it off. Putting it off means it is less likely to happen. Believe me when I tell you all sorts of things will pop up to distract you from taking care of yourself. Do not neglect yourself. Please, do not say you do not have time. This is something that requires you to make time. Think about that car with no gas. If you need to go somewhere and your tank is empty, you are not likely to pass the gas station and neglect getting gas. You're going to make time to make that stop. Apply that same principle to your life when it comes to self-care.

As we head into the next week, I urge you to feel encouraged. I spelled out encouragement below.

Embrace today while it is here. Try not to focus on the days ahead. Do not be afraid to just be in the moment. Is there someone who could use your undivided attention? Is there someone you'd like to spend some time with? Is there a friend that you have forgotten to call or check on?

Never give up. What is for you is for you. Sometimes success takes a lot of time. Do not be afraid to go further, nor dig deeper. You may be so close.

Care for yourself. Treat yourself with kindness and grace. It is important to pour into yourself. You're deserving of it.

Outdoors is what we need to get recentered sometimes. Do not just barricade yourself in the house. Get out of the house and enjoy some fresh air. Take a short walk and capture nature. Meditate on what you want.

Understand that we are a work in progress. Expect to make mistakes, and do not beat yourself down when you do. Learn from your mistakes and do better.

Reflect on who you are and where you are going. Please do not become complacent. It is important to have goals, dreams, and passion.

Apples are good for you (in most cases). Apples help maintain happiness from within.

Grace is so important in life's journey. We all need it at some point. Just as you have grace for others, please do not forget to extend it to yourself. None of us is perfect.

Excellence should be what you strive for, not perfection. Be the best you can be. Do what is right.

DAY 18

CONFRONT YOUR PROBLEMS

Don't run from your problems. Address them instead. If you keep running, you will find that you will always be running because your problems will keep chasing you. Failing to address them does not erase them. They just instill fear in you. Whatever it is, know that you can handle it. Stop running. Address it head-on responsibly. If this sounds familiar: it is. I previously said these things in the boundaries chapter. It applies there, and it applies here too. Problems generally do not just go away on their own. Well, some may, but for the most part, some action is required. Problems that you allow to linger will just keep showing up. Dealing with your problems in an effective manner helps. Running does not.

Why are you running away anyway, especially when the trouble will usually just follow you? Are you afraid? Are you a procrastinator? Are you not equipped to handle it? Do you just not know how to handle it? These may all be valid reasons for you to be running. But running gets tiring. You can only run for so long.

- Are you ready to stop?
- What is your problem?
- What are your challenges?
- Have you thought of solutions?
- Can these challenges be alleviated with a plan?
- What can you do to make things better?
- What has worked so far, and what hasn't?
- Are there resources available, and have you looked?
- Is there someone to help you if you need it?
- What happens if you do nothing?
- What happens if you do something?
- How important is resolving the matter to you?
- What is the problem costing you? (Your peace, time, etc.).

DAY 19

ANGER

Anger is a powerful emotion. While the feeling is negative, it is something we all have experienced. Many people feel psychologically aroused or triggered. Because the emotions invoked by anger can be so powerful, it is important that one is careful in their reaction. While anger in itself is a negative emotion, the feeling of being angry is not a bad thing. In fact, it can be a naturally appropriate response. However, one's reaction may not be appropriate.

Today, I want to briefly address reactions to anger. If you are a person who is quick to become angry, then know that isn't a good thing. Neither is it healthy. If you are a person who is quick to get angry, perhaps it is time to examine why. Are you easily triggered, manipulated, or unable to control your emotions? If you seem to get angry often, perhaps you have some unresolved issues or porous boundaries. Anger not be your go-to emotion for most things. It should be a rare emotion. If you feel like your daily routine is clothed with anger, please take a moment to reflect on what is causing this. Are you not content with your life? Are you not content with something that is happening in your life? Are you unhappy with the people around you? What can you do to make yourself less angry?

Now I know that anger will be an emotion that surfaces sometimes. When it happens, try to remain calm. Try not to rush to any conclusions. Perhaps examine what has happened, and think about the best way to respond. Try to keep a level head and think about how being angry is beneficial to you. Think about what you are feeling. Are you angry because you're hurt? Are you angry because your expectation has not been met? Are you angry because you feel disrespected? Are you angry because you're afraid? Are you angry because something was miscommunicated or misunderstood? What is the root of your anger?

Understanding what you're feeling and why may help you to respond more appropriately. In times of anger, one does not communicate effectively what is wrong or how one feels. A lot of times, anger interferes with communication. A lot of times, anger makes a situation worse.

DAY 20

DON'T SELF-DESTRUCT

Have you ever questioned your self-worth or your value? Have you allowed what others have said or done to you, to define you? Have you ever isolated yourself because you felt that you did not or do not belong? Have you ever told yourself that you are unlovable or undeserving of good things? Maybe you haven't had these exact thoughts, perhaps they were a different song, but had the same tune. I believe that as humans, we all have had thoughts that have consumed us, drained us, or even broke us all the way down. Very few people challenge the thoughts. Some people internalize everything that has ever happened to them. Some people do good at ignoring the thoughts in public, but find themselves still trapped by them in the comfort of their own privacy. Some people choose to drink away their problems, sleep away their problems, medicate their problems, drug up their problems, gamble away their problems, and or spend away their problems. Others use sex, food, pornography, television shows, working excessively, or any other vice to distract them from the pain that lingers inside. So yes, all these different forms may take the edge off momentarily, but the pain is not gone.

Sometimes people think that if they ignore or deflect the problem, they are winning. If you are one of these people, please know that you are not winning. You are losing. Also note that just because you are losing, it does not make you a loser. At any time, you can change your circumstances. You can change your outlook. Every day above ground is a day that you have opportunity. Even when it is cloudy outside, trust that clearer skies are in the forecast. If you find that every single day, it is cloudy, then perhaps it is time for you to move. You do not have to stay in something that steals your joy and or peace. I am not encouraging you to run when things get hard, but I am encouraging you to take responsibility for your position. Take responsibility for your own peace of mind. Take responsibility for your own happiness. If someone was just hitting you continuously in the face, are you just going to stand there and allow yourself to keep getting hit! If you happen to be a person who would just stand there and allow yourself to be subject to such pain, then I am very concerned for you. I am concerned that you do not value yourself. I would urge you to seek professional help as soon as possible. Nothing I say in this book is going to resonate with you, if you do not see any value in yourself. Please know I am not saying this to judge you or insult you: I am saying this because you need to hear it. You need to know it. You need to do something about it.

Our life is precious. I do not care who you are, where you work, who you know, or what has happened in your life up to now. None of that matters in deciding if your life is precious.

Understand how unique you are and understand that you have purpose. Even when family abandons you, your spouse leaves you, your friend betrays you, your co-workers gossip about you, your job fires you, strangers stare at you, or you feel like you have nothing or no one; remember that you're still valuable. It may not feel like it, but it doesn't make it untrue. These are the times when you have to rely on you. It may be scary. It may be uncomfortable. It may even feel so unfair. That is okay. If you give up on you, then who do you expect to have faith in you? I mentioned before that others have their own problems to tend to. You cannot expect that they have the capacity to carry you through. Sometimes you have to be your own cheerleader. You may have fallen, but if you are determined enough, you will get up. Maybe you have to lift to your knees first, but still that is progress. That beautiful mind of yours is so powerful. Often, we do not give it enough credit. It is more valuable than any computer or technology.

Self-destruction is not about what others do to you. It is what you do to yourself. Learn to be kind to yourself. Be in control of your own thoughts. Even when others have a lot to say about you, you can choose to accept or reject what is said. Sometimes it is good to hear what others have to say. There may be truth to it and it may not. Consider the source, the information, and how you want to proceed with it. Constructive criticism can be very valuable to you. Are you able to listen without being defensive? Are you able to sort through the information to determine what is useful and what is not? Are you able to keep the information you deem fits you and release the rest without feeling burdened? If you are able to do this, then you set yourself to becoming a better version of yourself.

If you find that you are often triggered or feel attacked when someone offers you advice, their opinion, constructive criticism, or feedback, perhaps you are not feeling secure in who you are as a person. We are all imperfect people, so we are bound to mess up, misunderstand, or need help at some point. That is not weakness. Being able to consider different perspectives, learn from others, be accountable for our mistakes, and allow ourselves to be corrected, is growth. I am not encouraging you to be passive or for you to accept any and all information that someone gives you. I am encouraging you to be openminded, less offensive, and receptive to ideas and feedback other than your own. Now if you have a fool in front of you that is insulting your intelligence or character, rather than argue or defend your stance, just walk away. There is no need to allow yourself to be disrespected or angered. Protect your peace when necessary.

Lastly, I want to encourage you to stop tormenting yourself with destructive thoughts. Please stop them at the root, so you do not end up with a tree of poison in your yard. Destructive thoughts are full of poison that ends up affecting your peace and joy, if you allow them to linger or grow. They never grow into a flower, no matter how much you water them. It only will cause discord and discontentment. There is no need for you to focus or revisit all the things that have ever went wrong in your life. "Negative thoughts will never produce a positive life" (author unknown). Stop giving power to what is dead in your life. It only lives because you are giving it power. Restructure your thoughts with things that uplift you and bring you joy. Be encouraged.

DAY 21

LETTING GO

At this moment, what are you holding onto? What are you still holding onto? What do you need to let go of that you have had a hard time pardoning? What things have you refused to accept? Sometimes we cannot move forward because we do not want to accept reality. We may be fighting with reason or understanding. We may be fighting with not feeling comfortable. We may be fighting with fear. We may be fighting with what was and not accepting what is. I am not here judging you. I am here trying to free you. The burden may be too heavy, and you will not just let it go. You may have an image you're trying to keep up with. You may have guilt that has you in bondage. You may be wrestling with a vision that has not panned out as you envisioned. Whatever it is, it is keeping you from progressing. Whatever it is, it is hurting you and not helping you.

How do you protect yourself from ongoing pain? Let whatever it is go. Sometimes you may not even have to let go, but maybe stop gripping so tightly. So often, we hold tight because we are busy trying to control every moment. Loosen that grip so you at least feel comfortable. You will begin to lose strength when you hold onto something so tightly. It takes so much to hold onto something with all your might. Eventually, you'll grow tired and be forced to let go. When you are forced to let go, that fall may hurt intensely. Don't let go because you are forced to. In reality, when you hold onto something so tightly, you really do not have much control at all. You may think you do because your brain wants to believe that. But truthfully, you have less control. You can try it now if you do not believe me. Take hold of an object and hold it with all your might, and see what happens. See how much control you really have and for how long. You'll end up dropping whatever it is after a little while.

TODAY, I ENCOURAGE YOU TO REFLECT ON THINGS, PEOPLE, OR circumstances that you need to loosen your grip on or simply let go of. Think about what holding on is costing you. Are you benefitting from it? Does holding on make sense? Are you suffering from it? How might your life differ if you let go? I challenge you to do what you need to do. Even if you're not ready to let go today, wrap your mind around doing so soon.

DAY 22

THE REFLECTION IN THE MIRROR

Hey, how are you doing today? How are you feeling? What is on your mind? As I ask these questions, take time to reflect and answer them. Of course, I cannot hear you. But you hear you. It is important to be self-aware. You know you best, so do not be afraid to dig into yourself. Dig deep. Healing comes from within. Yes, there may be circumstances around you that contribute to your discomfort or pain, but even if those circumstances were to be taken away, that does not automatically make you better. So when I ask how you are doing, answer honestly. It is important to check in with yourself. You do not have to wait for someone to ask you how you are doing or how you are feeling. A lot of times, people ask you without really caring what your response is. When asking someone how they are, they respond, "I'm okay, or I'm fine." A lot of people say that they are okay when they are not. But moving on, some people ask if one is okay just to greet; some do it to start a conversation, and some do it to be polite. I am not implying that everyone who asks you how you are, doesn't care. But I have found that many do not. Some even care but do not know what to do with the information if you tell them that you are not okay.

So when I ask how are you doing today, become comfortable with being honest. Even if you're not in the best mood, you can say that and still be positive. I am not saying that you must be. Here is an example of not feeling okay but being optimistically positive: "I am struggling right now, but I have faith that I will not bear this burden for long. I am looking forward to brighter days." This is much more positive than not feeling okay and then beating yourself up over it. Remember, even though it rains, the sun will come out again. But if you keep your blinds closed, how will you know when the sun begins to peak out? A part of life is accepting that bad things happen. However, a big part of having a good life is doing your part to take advantage and enjoy the good things. If you often look at the glass as half empty instead of half full, you are likely setting yourself up for failure. You have to motivate yourself much of the time. Do not have the expectation that everyone around you should be advocating for you or cheering for you. You have to be your own cheerleader. You have to learn to advocate for yourself. You must learn to enjoy life even when no one supports you. You have to learn to enjoy life even when things are not going according to your plan. Have some grace and be willing to be flexible. You're limiting yourself if you only look through life with a narrow lens. Sometimes it is appropriate to be open-minded. Sometimes it is appropriate to adjust or even adapt. That does not mean you have to change who you are completely. You're not a mold meant to remain the same over time. At some point, you should be evolving. At some point, you should see growth. Now do not rate your growth at the speed of someone else. You have to do what works for you. Stay in your own lane.

As we talk about the person you are and who you are becoming, I have another question for you. Please do not take offense because this is very direct. Are you standing in your own way? Are you the problem instead of the solution? Are you the person creating inner turmoil? Do you have peace within yourself? Are you making trouble for others? Are you at the center of the drama? Do you bring light or darkness to others? Are you judgmental? Are you a finger-pointer who blames everyone else and takes no accountability for your part? Do you listen, or are you always waiting to be heard? Did you get the memo that you are not perfect? We aren't even close to perfect, and I gather that neither of us will ever arrive there. So do not strive for perfection: instead, strive for excellence in all you do. Be willing to put forth your best every day. If you give your best, you never really fail. Don't worry about the things you cannot do; instead, put more focus on what you can do. You weren't designed to be able to do everything. That is why it is so important to stay in your lane. We all have different gifts, characteristics, perspectives, and skills. Embrace who you are…even while you are a work in progress.

Lastly, it is important that you be you. If you are self-destructive, then, of course, you do want to work through this. Try reflecting instead of deflecting. I am advocating that you stop being who you think you are supposed to be or what others want you to be. Stop pretending, and please do not fake it until you make it. That is not authentic. Be who you want to be; if that takes work, then do the work. No one is preventing you from being your best version except yourself.

DAY 23

FORGIVENESS

Many people struggle with forgiveness. If you find that forgiveness is something that is difficult for you, then just know you definitely are not alone. Forgiveness is more than just moving on. Forgiveness is not saying that the wrong done to you was okay. Forgiveness is about letting go and not holding on to the hurt. It is making peace within, so you no longer have to suffer. A part of this is releasing the person who has harmed you. It may be difficult to make peace. Much of the time, your pride is standing in the way. You may feel as if you are not prideful, but many times we are, even if we do not realize it. The part of you that wants to avenge, the part of you that feels slighted, the part of you that wants to be spiteful, the part of you that wants to reciprocate the pain, the part of you that is stubborn all comes down to your pride. It is very hard to let go and forgive when pride stands in the way,

Are you still harboring resentment or extreme anger toward someone else? Has someone wronged you, and you just can't let it go? Do you harbor hatred in your heart based on something someone has done to you? If so, what is stopping you from letting it go? Why do you hold on to it? Do you think if you do not hold on so tightly, you won't remember? Do you think that holding on keeps the person accountable? It does not. You're not that powerful. It is not up to us to make someone else accountable. God will handle that. It goes back to the fact that you cannot control anyone but yourself. When you hold on to pain and choose not to forgive, you are not hurting the other person. You are not punishing them. You are only punishing yourself. It is you that gets irritated or emotional when the person surfaces. It is you who does not have any peace because you are too busy thinking of the other person. You may be thinking of how much you cannot stand them. You may be thinking about how nothing good will come to that person. You may be thinking that the person is not worth forgiveness. However, it is your mind that is occupied with negative thoughts. It is your mood that has shifted. It is your peace that is disturbed. Meanwhile, the other person is living their life. That person is not basing their life decisions on you. It is likely that the person is not even thinking about you. So again, I ask, why are you entertaining someone who has wronged you? Either accept that they made a mistake and give them grace, or forgive and move on with your life. It makes no sense for you to make this an issue. It is of no benefit to you. You learn from the lesson and move forward. You do not have to keep company with the individual. You do not have to become a fool and turn a blind eye. It is okay to acknowledge that a wrong was done, and although you do not like it, you are not going to break. Someone may have really hurt you. You may think that what they have done is unforgivable. Remember that forgiveness does not mean you have to forget. It may not be the best idea to forget, but it is okay to accept what has happened and make peace with it.

Remember that holding on to hurt does not benefit you. It weighs you down. You are not hurting the person who wronged you by not forgiving. Forgiveness is about you. It frees you. It liberates you. But it is something that you have to do for yourself when you're ready. Be encouraged.

DAY 24

CHECK-IN

Happy day to you. How are you feeling? What are you feeling? Be honest with yourself. Are you thinking positively today? Have you forgiven? Have you practiced self-care?

Let's recap what we last covered. The subjects covered may have felt a bit heavy. These are the topics that many struggle with and find difficulty healing from. These topics were not surface-level stuff. It reached down and dug deep. Forgiveness, Letting Go, Anger, Don't Self-Destruct, Confronting Your Problems, and The Reflection In The Mirror may have caused you to explore deeper in your healing journey. Do not be afraid to revisit these subjects. They often take some time to work through.

NOW THAT THE OVERVIEW IS OUT OF THE WAY, LET US BE ON our way. It is day 24, and I am so proud of you for pressing through! There may have been some tough days, but you were resilient. You got through it. Also, be mindful that there will still be some trying days ahead. Know that it is okay and that you have what it takes inside of you to push through. You're strong, and you know it. You may be wondering why you always need to be strong. You may be tired of being strong. You may just want it to be somebody else's turn to be strong. Hopefully, you have someone in your life to provide you with some support sometimes. It may be important to voice your feelings or frustrations to those you rely on for support. If they do not know something is wrong, how can they help? If you aren't sharing your heart with them, they may not know how much you are hurting. Do not be afraid to open up to those who you care about. You shouldn't have to go through the storm alone. Ask for help if you need it. Please do not see asking for help as a weakness. Remember, we all need help sometimes. If you cannot find physical support, perhaps seek the help of a support group online.

Just one more week, and you will have completed a milestone. That should be exciting. Keep pushing; you are almost there.

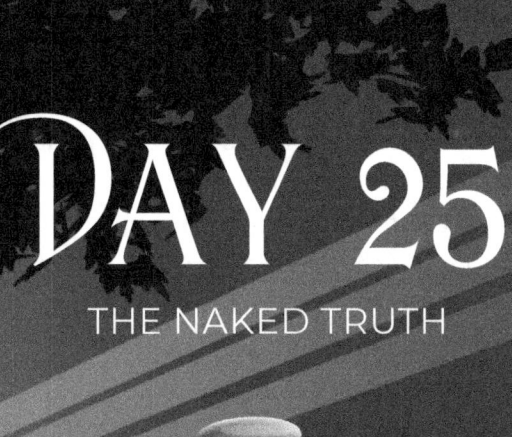

DAY 25

THE NAKED TRUTH

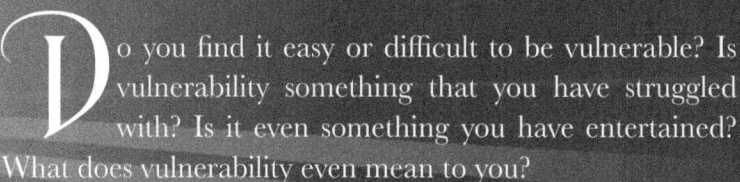

Do you find it easy or difficult to be vulnerable? Is vulnerability something that you have struggled with? Is it even something you have entertained? What does vulnerability even mean to you?

Let's take a moment to look deep within ourselves. I want you to look beyond your clothes. In fact, find a mirror. Take off every piece of clothing. Take off anything that hides you. Now look in the mirror as you stare at yourself naked. How does this feel? Does it feel comfortable or uncomfortable? Why? As you stare at yourself, breathe. Do not turn away. Do not judge how you look. Do not be ashamed. Do nothing but just look at the parts that make up you. Take your time. There is no need to rush. Examine the hairs on your head if you have hair. If you do not, examine the smoothness and shape of your head. Next, examine your beautiful eyes. You may see nothing special about them, nor beautiful, but it is you, so embrace you. It is beauty in being you. Now, look at your ears, nose, lips, and chin. Still beautiful, no matter the shape or size. Take a look at your neck. Feel your neck. Is there any tension there? Scan your body and look at each part before you. Think about how grateful you are to have all these moving body parts that work together to give life to you. Look at how each body part has its own function. The arm is not trying to be the leg, nor are the feet trying to be the hands. So remember this as you walk through life. You do not have to be anyone but yourself. You have your own function, your own responsibilities, your own values, and your own destiny.

Now that you have stared at your naked body, do you feel a sense of more closeness to yourself? Are you proud of the person who stands before you? Are you angry or disappointed at the person staring back at you? Do you feel sorry for that person? Do you feel grace? Do you feel love? Do you even like this person? Do you feel connected to this person or estranged? If you feel estranged, what do you need to do to repair it? What do you need to do to reunite yourself? Do you need to forgive yourself? I am asking so many questions, hoping you will be able to answer. I cannot tell you exactly what you need to do within yourself, but I trust that you do. Why? Because you know you best. You know what makes sense for you and to you. You know your struggles. You know your pain. You know your successes and losses. You know your strengths and your weaknesses. You have an idea of what changes need to be made. Dig deep, and know that the answer is there. You may not like the answers, and that is okay. Just because you do not like the truth does not make it false. It does not mean you get a pass. You still have to press forward and do the groundwork. Do not expect someone else to do it for you because no one can do it but you. Do not expect a miracle. Be reasonable, and be willing to do the work a little at a time.

What is your truth? What lies have you told others or even yourself? What does lying do for you? Is it really working? It may shield you at the moment or camouflage your truth, but deep down, those lies are destroying you. What sense is living when you are not living in your own truth? In some regard, you have created a fictional character in a story. It is not your story if it is based on someone you don't even know. Be you, even if it means you will not be popular. Be you even if it means fewer people will like you. I would personally rather someone accept me for who I am. If you do not like who you are, become who you want to be. Work on being better while embracing who you are right now. I firmly believe we are all a work in progress. I do not like everything about me, but I do like me. There are some things I have just come to accept that may never change, but there is so much of me that is becoming better. I am only improving because I am doing the work to improve. I cannot do anything at all and expect progress to be made. Neither can you. Sometimes we have these unreasonable expectations. Please check and ensure that your expectations are reasonable in this journey. Also, know that you do not often have to reinvent the wheel. Do your research. Open up your circle and be willing to learn from others. Consider having a mentor in your life. You need someone who cares for you and is not afraid to be truthful with you. Find ways you can self-improve. Do not be afraid to ask for help from others sometimes. None of us can make it in this world alone. Human connections are important. I encourage you to do what you need to do. This is your life, and you're responsible for it.

DAY 26

ENOUGH IS ENOUGH

Breathe; it is going to be okay. You may be wondering how you are supposed to heal and how long this process takes. Know that you're not alone in how you feel. It may have only been days that you find yourself hurting. You may be past the days' stage, and it has now been several weeks. Perhaps you are beyond weeks, and the months are passing by. Maybe you have been hurting for years, and the pain is still present. You may be asking what you can do to ease this burden. You may wonder if there is light at the end of the tunnel. You may be tired of this whole healing process and just want to feel better. Feeling better may not even feel within reach.

Some of you may ask how you can be productive during this difficult time. You may be so overwhelmed with wrestling with your own thoughts. You may have pacified yourself with vices of your choice. You may have begun working to heal, yet you are still hurting. Although you may feel so many emotions, please understand that this is still a part of the healing process. You may have to heal in layers. Healing is not a band-aid approach. The band-aid does not cure the wound—it simply covers it. You are doing the work beyond the surface. You are trying to heal the parts that people cannot see. So it is going to take time. The trauma you have endured does not just magically disappear. So do not be looking for a magic wand. A part of healing is sitting in pain. We naturally want to expedite this step. It is uncomfortable. It is scary. It is not pleasing. We want to run away from it. But running away just leads to prolonged pain. Running away may delay pain temporarily, but trust me, it will be back. So while it is here, accept it, and be willing to work through it. Feel what you feel, so eventually, you won't feel like you do now. Face what went wrong. Face what went right. Face your faults. Face your loss. Face your mistakes. Face your lessons. Face your disappointment. Face yourself and the demons that live within you. Without you facing your truth, you will never fully heal.

DAY 27

FIND THE LIGHT

We are aware that life happens to all of us. We are going to have good days, and we are going to have bad days. It is difficult to appreciate the good days without ever experiencing any bad ones. Sometimes our bad experiences humble us. Sometimes our bad experiences cause us to hurt. Sometimes life can even seem so unfair. There are bad things that have happened to me that I did not deserve. However, there were also good things that happened to me that I did not deserve. I am often reminded of God's grace amid my troubles. I encourage you to reflect on the grace upon you as you navigate life's journey. If you choose to focus only on the negative things you have endured, it is unlikely that you will have a positive life. Consider focusing on the good things that have happened. Give more weight to those moments, so you have a glass half full rather than a glass half empty approach.

As you heal, you may be wondering how you end up here. You may be beating yourself up about the mistakes you have made. In some regard, you may feel foolish. You may even just be frustrated with yourself and your situation. It is life: stuff is going to happen. Learn from your mistakes. Find the lessons in every situation. If you are just experiencing and not learning along the way, then that may be a huge problem. There comes a point in your life when you should be tired of running in the same circle. That circle has no destination. Once again, you're like the hamster on the wheel, just running but going nowhere. It is up to you to do better. It is up to you to pull on your bootstraps and formulate some kind of plan. At this juncture, you should not just be taking the day as it comes. You have to put in the effort. You have to discipline yourself. You have to motivate yourself. You have to believe in yourself. You have to know what you want or at least know what you do not want. I encourage you to do something rather than sit there and do nothing at all. Try. If you happen to fall, dust yourself off and get back up fast. There is no need to lay in your sorrows. Remember, I will give you a day to mope and feel sorry for yourself. But tomorrow, you wipe those tears away and smile. Maybe you do not have it in you to smile about your future just yet but smile because you are alive and full of opportunities out there. If you do not believe in yourself, how can you expect anyone else to do so?

So where is the light? I would gather it is away from the darkness. You've likely met people in your life that are full of light. They are there encouraging, cheering people on, giving hope, being supportive, willing to help, etc. These people are scattered about, and they may seem to be few, but know they are still out there. When you find the light, move toward it. Absorb it so that light can shine within you. That light gives hope. It gives purpose. It gives grace. That light is comforting and peaceful. Do not be afraid of the light. For some, the light can be intimidating. It can be different from the norm but know it is a good thing. The light is your friend.

Speaking of light, if your home is dark inside, draw back the curtains and let the sun in. It is not good to be surrounded by darkness so much unless you're sleeping or winding down. Sometimes it is good to just step outside and enjoy some fresh air as well. It is important to lighten your mood and do things that help bring out the best version of you.

DAY 28

WHAT DO YOU NEED

You're almost at the finish line of your thirty-day healing journey. Now at this point, it does not mean you are fully healed. If you are fully healed, then I salute you. For the majority, though, I suppose you still have work to do. Do not be afraid of the work that still needs to be done. You are capable of getting it done. Remember, the healing journey is not a race. You have to go at your own pace.

So at this juncture, what is it that you need? What is going to allow you to get to the finish line? What do you need to be the best you? What do you need to add, delete, or redo? Are there changes in your life that you need to make? Are there areas that have been discussed here that you need to revisit? What do you need to keep going? What is going to motivate you? What do you need to survive? What can you not live without? What are your distractions? What do you need to improve? What do you need to move forward?

I know I have posed several questions, but I have more. It is important that you ask yourself these questions. It is important that you answer the questions. Is it time to get resources? Do you need an accountability partner? Do you have a mentor? Who do you look up to? Who are you learning from? It is important to surround yourself with people you can learn from. It is important to have growth. If you are not learning, how can you grow?

I hope this chapter has caused you to consider what it is that you need. Once you figure out what you need, please consider how you can obtain what you need. After you do that, put forth a plan to get there. When that is done, execute it. Be encouraged.

DAY 29

HAPPINESS

Happiness is something that we all want. I have never heard a person say that they did not want happiness. I have heard many say that they are not happy or they have a difficult time achieving happiness. I believe that happiness is a state of mind. While happiness is one's own responsibility, there are different things that allow it to happen. I guess the main thing is that one has to be open to it. Happiness is not perfection. Happiness is what one feels inside. What makes you happy? Stop for a moment and reflect on the many things that make you happy. When was the last time you felt happy? If it has been a while, why is that? Are you careful not to base your happiness on what others do? Now other people and the relationships we have with them may contribute to our happiness, but another person on their own merit does not create happiness within us. No one else is responsible for your happiness. It is your job to create your own happiness. It is important not to allow others to define happiness for you. Happy can be what you want it to be. It does not have to fit inside a box. It is what you make it.

If you find that you lack happiness, what can be done to change that? What is contributing to your unhappiness? What do you need to remove or add to your life to feel happiness? This could be things or even people. Maybe your job is causing you so much stress, and you feel like this is really weighing you down and causing unhappiness. If this is the case, what can you do within your reach to change this? You do have choices. I am not advocating that you should quit because you're not happy. I am not advocating that you stay somewhere you're not happy, either. I am saying that you have a say in your life. Leaving your job may not be an option, but setting some boundaries at work may improve your contentment. Maybe addressing the challenges at work may make being there more comfortable. Maybe reaching out to management to discuss things that are hindering you from working efficiently may be an option. Perhaps going back to school to pursue something different or allow advancement may be an option. Maybe searching for a new job in a place where you feel valued is an option. Maybe working somewhere that allows you to pursue your passion instead of just working somewhere that is financially better can help you feel happier. Perhaps working for yourself instead of having a boss micromanaging you may be an option. I do not know your situation, but I do know that you always have choices.

Perhaps you aren't happy because you stopped having fun. When was the last time you had fun? When was the last time you made time for fun? Fun is required to have a balanced life. Fun is not just for children. If you are not having fun, then why not? What is stopping you? You. It is imperative that you begin making time to have fun. I encourage my clients to plan activities that they enjoy. I think having a fun activity on your agenda at least monthly is necessary. If you can do it more, do so. The absence of fun contributes to unhappiness.

What do you even like to do for fun? Do not tell me what you used to do ten years ago. Tell me what you do for fun now. Maybe you do not know because it has been so long. Maybe it is time to venture out and even try new things. It is okay to even do those things you did ten years ago. Just make time for it. I challenge you to plan out an activity for you to enjoy within the next month. You can choose to do something with others or even by yourself. The thing about others is that sometimes they cancel. Do not allow them to cancel plans to ruin the fun for you. Perhaps always have a plan B.

DAY 30

30-DAY HEALING JOURNEY
COMPLETED

Facing the naked truth, enough is enough, finding the flight, determining what you need, and happiness were the last chapters covered. Those were some heavy things there. You may still be processing some things or even still trying to work through them. Those last chapters may take time to resonate with you. They may have brought some insight. Hopefully, they helped you in some way.

How are you feeling right now? I hope you are filled with joy and much peace. You have reached the end of the 30-day milestone. Isn't this exciting! Do you feel accomplished? Are you proud of yourself? Well, know that I am proud of you for this amazing accomplishment. You persevered and stuck with it. You did the work that you needed to do to get better. Celebrate this accomplishment. Please do not stop here. Continue healing. This was just the beginning. Your best days are ahead of you. You haven't even met your best self yet.

As you move on, just be mindful of what has been covered. Work through your trauma, troubles, and frustrations with a positive attitude. Acknowledge your faults and learn from your lessons. Ensure you are not standing in your own way. If you find yourself stuck, seek out resources. Do not be afraid to talk with someone about your pain. It is important to release so you do not blow up or shut down. Imagine yourself as a balloon. If you keep holding everything inside, the balloon will continue to expand. It will get bigger and bigger until it eventually pops. Do not allow this to happen to you. You can prevent this by releasing it.

Also, remember that you can always revisit a chapter if you feel you need to. I actually recommend it. As time goes by, it may become difficult to remember everything you have gone over. As life happens, you'll become distracted and find yourself repeating some old bad habits. Revisiting the chapters will act as a refresher or maybe even just maintenance.

I wish you the best and hope this book benefits you in your healing journey. Be encouraged. You got it from here.

ABOUT THE AUTHOR

Jen (Jennifer) Nicole is a Michigan native. Her first passion is writing. She prefers writing fiction over non-fiction, allowing her to express herself vividly and creatively. In addition to writing, she finds joy in helping others. Jen bleeds compassion. You can see this in her life experiences and work as a professional counselor. Jen's goal is to save the world one person at a time. She believes that this particular book will help millions of people in their self-healing journey.